Well, I Think So!

DOLLY SCHUFFMAN

© Copyright 1984 by Dolly Schuffman

Library of Congress
Catalog Card Number: 84-071669

Designed by Dolly Schuffman

ISBN Number: 0-931243-00-9

First Printing 1984

Published in the
United States of America

DART PUBLISHING COMPANY
19344 Wyandotte Street, Suite 122
Reseda, California 91335

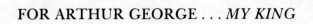

FOR ARTHUR GEORGE . . . *MY KING*

If one believes in love and respect
Believes in caring and friendship
Experiences the joys of sharing
But most of all,
Believing that the combination
Of all these things
Is what makes living worth-while,
Then they've found the secret of contentment.

— Dolly Schuffman

To Help You Select Entertainment
That Stimulates The Mind
This Poetic *TABLE OF CONTENTS*
Will Help You In Your Find.

We start with a known expression,
One everybody knows.
If someone asks you if they're right,

Well,
I
Think
So!

WELL, I THINK SO!

It's Evasion, no Persuasion
And assumes many things.
What's the expression we all know?
"Do you think I'm right?"

Well, I think so!

Who's to say who's right or wrong?
Who's to say who's big or strong?
What's the expression we all know?
"Do you think I'm right?"

Well, I *Think* So!

Who's to say just dress in blue?
Who's to say if my age is true?
What's the expression we all know?
"Do you think I'm right?"

Well, I Think So!

Who's to say if she's too fat?
Who's to say just leave him flat?
What's the expression we all know?
"Do you think I'm right?"

Well, *I* Think So!

Who's to say these rhymes aren't good?
You'd write your own, if you thought you could!
What's the expression we all know?
"Do you think I'm right?"

Well, I Think *So!*

So keep on thinking, 'cause as you read
Poems give meaning to your need.
What's the expression we all know?
"Do you think I'm right?"

Well, I Think So!

A VOICE

I hear a voice
Down deep within
It hums Life's tune
Begin . . . Begin.

The beauty
Of it all explodes
And charges me
With doing.

A little here
A little there
For life
I am pursuing!

A FAMILY TREE

The trunk was us,
You and me.
One branch sprang up
And we were three.

Another came
And we were four.
A tree of love
Forevermore.

We watched and nurtured
Every branch.
So soon they flowered
And took their stance.

As they matured
Reached out and mated,
You and I,
We were elated.

Their seeds of love
Soon bore sweet fruits.
We felt great joy
Down to our roots.

How proud the trunk,
You and me,
As we hold up
Our family tree.

WHO IS SHE?

She's a helper
She's a mother
She's a teacher
She's a friend.

She did guide him
She did raise him
She did show him
She did lend.

How you treat her
When you meet her
Could reveal
Your character flaw.

Be gracious
When you greet her,
She could be
Your mother-in-law!

LIFE'S REPETITION

What you see was seen before.
What you feel was felt.
That is life's repetition,
The cards your ancestors dealt.

They're in your hands for a lifetime.
Too soon, you'll pass the deal.
It's a game with responsibility,
Played right, it has appeal.

There's power in dealing down
To the children coming up.
If you want some changes, redeal!
It shouldn't be a matter of luck.

There will be payments on demand
When your children pick up their cards.
This is life's repetition
Stack their deal so it's not too hard.

I PLEDGE

I pledge allegiance
To my loves,
As long as I shall live.

One pulls me right,
One pulls me left,
My soul to them I give.

As one of them has aptly said,
"Your time between us
Runs so thin."

As long as God,
Loves them so,
He should have made me twins!

EQUAL TIME FOR SPRING

HE SAID:

Equal time for dark and light.
Equal time to set your sights.
Objectives planned and neatly done.
Equal time to plan for fun!

SHE SAID:

What's this equal time you see?
It's for everyone but me!
Sure, you plan the days ahead . . .
I do the work . . . you're still in bed!

HIS GIFT

He gave me a gift
So precious and new,
To share with the ones
Who are worthy and true.

He gave me a heart,
He gave me a soul
To help me be brave,
To help me be bold.

He talked of his dreams
And what soon shall pass.
How life is so precious
We must make it last.

So I'll shine like the sun
And glow in the night.
I'll hold to my values
And never lose sight.

I'll feel what I see,
Not fear the unknown.
I'll absorb all the knowledge
From those who have grown.

I'll learn to take chances.
At least, I'd have tried.
Not defeated if wrong
In that, there is pride!

He gave me a heart
And gave me a soul.
Also laughter and trust
And a mind to unfold.

I wasn't promised
The best that there is.
But I will not question
The will that is *His*.

And when he calls out,
"It's time now to go."
I shall be ready
And willing I know.

For I will live on
In the hearts I have touched.
For the caring and loving,
Compassion and such.

My soul will return
(It's the insight I've got)
In the form of another
To fill my blank spot.

He gave me a gift
So precious and new,
To share with the ones
Who are worthy, like you!

RHYMES OF THE TIMES

Today's what's in is tomorrow's what's out!
But given enough years between,
There occurs a fad turnabout,
Styles come back in time, it seems.

Woman's Lib has been a turnabout.
Is being free such a big deal?
We have the kids, we go to work.
We still clean, we still shop and fix meals.

We bought our TVs for entertainment.
Have you seen the news lately?
It isn't easy to be amused by,
Brokow, Brinkley and Blakely.

Fashions are amusing, though.
I shopped last week to find,
I felt I'd slept a hundred years
And awoke in another time.

The important thing is to be well read.
Newspaper details are so sordid.
Paperbacks are more our speed,
With covers flashy and torrid.

The theater is in, but tickets cost.
But so nice to be on the scene.
To add that touch of success,
Why not hire a white limousine!

We know the air is not so good.
How long can you hold your breath?
If we don't really clean the air,
What on earth will there be left?

Our times really make our rhymes
Full of mysteries and riddles.
So let's all join in harmony
While government just fiddles.

*

The best way you will ever find
To keep your soul alive
Is to always speak with ease and truth
It's important that you try . . . and . . .

TALK TO YOUR GRANDCHILDREN

Let them know just what you think, with
Your chain of thoughts as loving links.

Explain what is and what could be —
When dues aren't paid, 'cause nothing's free!

Tell them you're a person, too.
Let them know all sides of you.

Be their guide, they'll understand
As you're walking hand in hand.

TALK TO YOUR GRANDCHILDREN

Stories told will make them thrive.
Their heritage gives children pride.

Keep harsh tones low, don't intimidate.
A loving voice will always rate.

Plan the times to be together.
Seeing, touching makes it better.

Then, make it clear that it's a pact
That, you'll tune in as they talk back!

GOOD LUCK

Good luck
Like the telephone,
Always rings
When you're not home.

Good luck
Weaves, its power bends.
It scoots around
Among your friends.

Good luck
Finds the other guy.
So many times
It passes by.

Good luck
Comes and goes away.
It's fickle —
'Cause it never stays.

Good luck
You say with your goodbyes,
In hopes
Luck will be satisfied.

Good luck's
Something we all yearn,
Maybe soon,
You'll have your turn!

GARBAGE

Garbage can be thrown by words
from thoughts that hurt our senses.
Not the kind put in paper bags
or tossed in cans near fences.

That kind of trash in paper bags
is kinder than you think.
The garbage spewn from human words
should be ground up in the sink!

WITH STYLE

I may have come
Into this world
With a butt
All shiny and new!
I may have come
Upside down,
With my skin
A hue of blue.

But when I go
Out of this world.
My memories
I'll pile.
I'll tie them up
Nice and neat
And leave this world
With Style . . .

DIFFERENT KIDS

A kid's a joke,
A kid's a goat,
Kids are children
Who need rope.

A kid has springs,
A kid has wings,
When kids are near,
It's love they bring.

All kids love life,
All kids know strife.
They're eager but
Not too polite.

Some kids are tall,
Some kids are small.
The noiseless ones
Are best of all.

PHONE CALL

I pushed down hard on the buttons,
Trying to call home.
But all I got was a buzzing sound
On the company telephone.

The buttons just weren't working.
Again and again I tried.
No phone would get the better of me,
It was a matter of pride!

I stopped to figure what was wrong.
When, suddenly, came a gleam —
The buttons I'd been pushing
Were on the adding machine!

THE THEME OF LIFE

In our childhood and teens —
The expanse of time seemed so vast,
We thought each year would never pass.

In our twenties —
That was when we developed dreams.
They were slow to show, too young it seems.

In our thirties —
Our world materialized
As plans we'd made were realized.

In our forties —
We saw the fruits of our endeavors.
Deciding then to live forever!

In our fifties —
Life's work we saw as justified.
So many tasks were qualified.

In our sixties —
We have time to remember our
20s, 30s, 40s, and 50s!

BABY SPEAKS

How strange the life you think you have
can be changed by such degree.
You hide emotions better hid
it's been the only way to be.

But as you gaze upon my face
emotions stir within,
For I'm a generation new
the circle now begins.

So soon you'll watch me take life's steps
with tender love and care.
We'll share the times I falter
but I'll know that you are there.

For you'll be special in my life
as special as can be.
Grandmothers are so wonderful,
and I chose you for me!

WHOSE CHILDREN ARE THEY?

Whose children are they
when they cry in the night?
Whose children are they,
who quiets their fright?

Whose children are they
when starved for affection?
Whose children are they,
who gives them direction?

Whose children are they
when there is a fight?
Whose children are they,
who sets them to right?

Whose children are they
when smoking some pot?
Whose children are they,
who tells them to stop?

Whose children are they
when kicked out of school?
Whose children are they,
who lays down the rules?

Whose children are they
when stealing's a thrill?
Whose children are they,
who curses their will?

Whose children are they
when seduced by a bum?
Whose children are they
when pregnancy comes?

Whose children are they,
who aches for lives tossed?
Whose children are they,
who cries for the loss?

Whose children are they?
That's easy to find.
Sometimes they're yours
and sometimes they're mine!

Respect the children in your home
Remember they're just there on loan.

SOMEONE ELSE'S KID

Someone else's kid is normal
His parents knew their job.
I look around to see my kid
the epitome of slob!

Someone else's kid is normal
His thank you's ring a bell.
I've tried with mine, believe me,
it's been a living hell!

Someone else's kid is normal
His report card says it, too.
Perhaps I'd better try again
to improve my point of view.

Someone else's kid is normal
I've never seen him late.
I look around to see my kid
he's swinging on a gate!

Someone else's kid is normal
How fast he grew up, they say.
My kid still scouts the neighborhood
seeking other kids to play.

Someone else's kid is normal
But to me the shining light
Reflects in my kid's loving eyes
when we hug and kiss goodnight!

When you mention what you hear
Be sure of facts going ear to ear!

CHANGING PLACES

If I were you
And you were me,
Would it change
Our destinies?

Advice you give,
You think is great,
With words you try
To guide my fate.

If I were you
And you were me,
Would you like
Advice that's free?

I'd gladly give
You words and yet,
You'd never change,
Not on a bet!

FUNNY BONE

Funny things
that make us laugh,
Embarrassment or
A fall called Prat!

An infant babe
who wears a frown.
A clown who has
his pants fall down.

Birds who speak
and dogs who smile.
Front teeth missing
from a child.

Friends blow bubbles
back to back,
Bubble gum bursts
and there's a laugh!

That horse you bet
staying out 'til dark.
That office gag
that fell apart!

Halloween costumes,
picnic races.
Whipped-cream pies
smashed on their faces.

On a summer's day
to keep real cool,
Your dog is swimming
in your pool.

Sure-fire laughter
from your lips.
A guy on skates
who slips and flips.

The very thing
that bald men dread,
A bird in flight
drops on your head!

Unfunny things
like funny bones,
When hit direct
can make you groan!

Ms. LADY LIFE

Lady Life is pleasant enough,
She spreads both good and bad.
She never means to give you strife
Nor even make you sad.

Like every kind of lady,
She is prone to change her mind.
She likes to give us ups and downs,
Knowing we'll be fine.

Lady Life is pleasant enough,
She gives time to set our goals.
She watches us pursue through life
Those dreams that we've been sold.

Lady Life is still maturing,
She tries to keep it mild.
She took her training from the best,
Being Mother Nature's child!

IT'S ALWAYS

It's always
A special time.
A special place
When my friends meet
Face to face.

It's always
A special look,
A special laugh
As tales unfold
Back to back.

The clock ticks on
But we don't care.
Forever young,
Let time beware!

It's always
A special date,
A special power
Of birthday joy,
Our happy hour.

PICTURE THIS

There's nothing to imagination,
Everybody has it.
Once you've learned how to use it,
It becomes a natural habit.

Just think the things you want to have
And they'll become available.
All you do is picture it,
To attain the unattainable.

Partial memories can start you off
It's easy as can be.
Your mind's eye forms the pictures
That seek out realities.

Imagine you're flying over treetops
Below there is the world.
It's time to land and look around
Imagination starts to whirl.

There are gigantic trees
In springs full bloom,
Bowing low with each heavy breeze.
And birds playing their courting games
With chirping sounds that tease.

Now see a swarm of butterflies,
They're playing hide and seek
While dancing through green foliage,
Their colors bright and neat.

Think hiking through a wooded glen,
And see what nature stores.
Stroll in beautiful and natural land,
Mark a path and claim it yours.

Pretend a dawn walk along the beach,
White foam blanketing the shore.
See ocean waves hitting shoreline rocks
And footprints on sandy floors.

Stop to collect seashells,
Feel glad you are alive.
Breathe deep and stretch
Looking far beyond . . .
Now resume a healthy stride.

See a handsome male, looking eye to eye,
At a sweet young girl, so frail.
This time I'll leave it up to you,
"Picture This," and finish the tale!

POOR ME AT THREE

It's great when you are
only '2',
When hugs and kisses
come to you.

The girls next door
now that I'm '3',
Never seem to see
it's me!

There's this sister
I sort of ordered.
How'd I know
that they'd adore her.

I know I'm still
the same sweet me,
But only sister
can they see.

I miss their hugs
and their kisses.
I regret the times
that I resisted.

I cry a lot
and say "poor me."
Who needs a sister
when you're '3'?

At night I pray
and ask the Lord
To make them hug me
when I'm '4'.

I'm suffering . . .
Why can't mommy see
It isn't easy
being '3'?

Know what I'm hoping
when I'm '4'?
That mommy has
No kids, no more!

WHEN

You know you're getting older *when*
It doesn't matter what applies.
When getting older simply means
You're learning to survive!

You know you're getting older *when*
What's called music offends your ears.
When you choose movies just for laughs
And not for splashing tears.

You know you're getting older *when*
You are always sure you're right.
When you never try to read a book
Without a bright side light.

You know you're getting older *when*
People's names just come and go.
When you'd rather be in sunny lands
Instead of ice and snow.

You know you're getting older *when*
You talk to yourself out loud.
When you'd rather not go at all,
Than be in a crushing crowd.

You know you're getting older *when*
All half truths you see right through.
When you know the one important thing
Is to have love returned to you.

You know you're getting older *when*
Credit cards fill up your purse.
When you always want to be on time,
For your Doctor to take you first!

You know you're getting older *when*
You stop dressing just for fads.
When you like less space to live in
And TV dinners aren't so bad!

THE DAUGHTER

This is the daughter
That everyone should have.
She's wonderful, delightful,
A lover of jazz.

She talks with her eyes,
She waves with her hands.
She wants what she wants,
She asks, not demands.

She's clever, inventive,
A beauty of sorts.
She never holds grudges,
She's wild about sports.

She plans for her future.
She'll never deny
That living with her
Really takes quite a guy.

She always will listen
When there are complaints.
She's strong in her beliefs,
Her feelings aren't faint.

She's quick to receive
Any message of heart.
She never backs off
From community parts.

She's tender and loving
And nurtures her child.
Deny her her voice
And she really goes wild.

This is my daughter
In case you didn't know.
It's not that I'm bragging,
It's pride that I show.

GLORIOUS THREE

If you have three friends
That you enjoy,
Here is a puzzle
That you can employ.

Sit at a table
With wine that's been poured.
Just you and your friends,
A total of four.

Now each tips their glass
And takes a good look.
True friendship is called,
Love, with no hook!

Though you're facing each other,
Four friends are not four.
You're a 'Glorious Three',
I'll explain, there is more.

Just look to your right
From the table that's square.
Then look to the left
And become now aware . . .

Number Three is so lucky
To those who relate.
It comes from tradition
To all of good faith.

Though you are still four,
Three best friends, you've each.
To prove what I mean,
Spread both arms and reach!

With reflections of love,
Each friend now can see
That the puzzle is solved.
There's your 'Glorious Three'.

HONESTY

Women sweet and women dear,
Change as the years go by.
Demands we make, seem extreme,
And we're hard to satisfy.

Some little things do set us off.
It's change of life, they say.
Our sense of humor dwindles,
We forget from day to day.

Like, everything is an emergency
And we don't want to wait.
It's harder to solve problems
And stay calm when someone's late.

We thought of others before ourselves,
So now, it is our turn.
Respect given is what we ask.
With patience, you could learn!

A TOAST TO FRIENDS

Friends don't come in packages and
Friends don't come in labels.
Friends are friends because they are,
It's friends who keep you stable.

Friends don't ask for reasons and
Friends don't ask you why.
Friends are friends because they are,
And because they are, you try.

You try to live the golden rule,
You try to not tempt fate.
You try to keep an open mind,
You try to keep your faith.

Friends just always understand
When you bend a rule.
And friends just always understand
When you play the fool.

Friends don't ever look
And then just turn away.
Because there are such things as friends,
I thank the Lord each day.

Since the beginning of Creation
Power and guilt stir motivation.

TUNING IN

The sexy time in TV land,
Starts every day at 12:00.
The television plays away
And into life it delves.

I often think how sad it is
To get hooked on a soap.
And how some people let themselves
Revolve around its scope!

They remember who has slept with whom
And who seduced the maid.
They sit before the TV screen
And root when someones laid!

Getting "turned on," as they say,
Means "tuning in" for some.
For me, I've found a better way
To get my sexual fun!

WHEN I WAS YOUNG

When I Was Young

> We played in streets
> along the neighborhood.
> And drivers always stopped for us,
> we knew they always would.

When I Was Young

We walked to school,
meeting friends along the way.
And after school, we'd meet again,
deciding where to play.

When I Was Young

Our days were spent
all summer in the park.
Parents never even cared
if we stayed out 'til dark.

When I Was Young

Things looked so good,
worms and snakes were great!
Pansies, daisies soft to touch,
butterflies, in their escape.

When I Was Young

We loved to dance,
at parties we would show,
We didn't drink or even smoke,
and "no" was always no!

When I Was Young

On grassy lawns,
we watched the clouds roll by.
Lying on our backs we'd fantasize,
mixing dreams with shapes and sky.

Life Was So Simple

When I was young,
we really had it made.
Too bad that all had to change,
I pity kids today.

TRUTH

She touched the world
and it recoiled.
It touched her
then she was soiled.

Ideals were stricken,
one by one
Still every day
she took her fun.

How simple truth,
it has such power.
But still she built
a falsehood tower.

Still she seeks
but cannot find,
Purity lost,
from her heart and mind.

FACING IT

The Doctor was handing her the pictures
Of the lines that now had formed.
They came from years of experience
Since her children had been born.

His camera, no doubt, was special.
Each and every flaw was revealed.
Magnifying hills and deep valleys.
The sight made her senses reel.

She questioned the pictures from the camera.
Could she really look like that?
She never thought she looked too bad,
She doubted the print-up fact!

It was then that she picked up a mirror
Relieved at what she did see.
Facing her was the face she knew,
No print-up was there, just she!

Suddenly, the bad time was over.
She really didn't mind what she saw.
So what if her face wasn't perfect,
Doesn't everyone have minor flaws?

Well, Nature moves in some funny ways,
'Cause the problem she didn't know —
She really needed glasses badly
So, in her eyes, the lines never showed!

A TIE FOR STANLEY

Open House was held on a Sunday
In the garden from 2 to 6.
A present for Stanley's retirement
Kept her emotionally mixed.

Deciding a tie would be perfect
She chose one she felt was quite right.
The stripes were in line with the side seams,
The colors were wonderfully bright!

Telling her mate of her purchase
She waited to hear how he felt.
"A tie on a rack can be handy", he said
"If you're planning to hang yourself."

Swiftly he opened the package.
"This is a tie to adore?"
"How much, my dear, were you paid,
To take this out of the store?"

On the day of celebration,
She went over early to help.
She thought of the gift she'd brought
And then how badly she felt.

She decided before Stanley opened it
That confession was good for the soul.
Taking Stanley aside, before guests arrived,
To him her tie story she told.

Then they both heard the ring of the bell
And in came a man with a fern.
Stanley got up and reached for the card.
He read it and laughingly turned.

"The card's from your husband
And he can't stop by."
"This plant is for me,
And you'll never guess why."

She grabbed for the card
To the answer to why . . .
It said,
"Plant this in your garden, and bury the tie."

MOLLY'S LITTLE PEARL

Here is a simple story
That always makes me laugh.
The mother's name is Molly,
She recalled some funny facts . . .

Molly came home from the hospital
With a new babe in her arms.
Her 2-year-old Pearl, ran and hugged hello,
A child with winning charms.

Molly's new infant was screaming,
Little Pearl gave the blanket a pat.
She looked up at Molly saying,
"Is 'IT' going to keep screaming like that?"

Molly found words of comfort,
Little Pearl seemed to settle back.
But now was the time to feed the babe,
It was hungry, and that's a fact.

As Molly was nursing the baby,
Little Pearl gave the blanket a pat.
She looked up at Molly saying,
"Is 'IT' going to keep eating like that?"

Molly found words of comfort,
Little Pearl seemed to settle back.
But now it was time to change the babe,
It had dirtied, and that's a fact.

Molly was changing the diaper,
Little Pearl gave the blanket a pat.
She looked up at Molly saying,
"Is 'IT' going to keep smelling like that?"

Molly found words of comfort,
Little Pearl seemed to settle back.
But now it was time to lay the babe down,
It was tired, and that's a fact.

Molly was covering the infant,
Little Pearl gave the blanket a pat.
She looked up at Molly saying,
"Is 'IT' going to keep sleeping like that?"

Again there were words of comfort,
Giving Molly's tummy a pat,
"If you're sure that it's sleeping," she said
"Just hurry and put 'IT' back."

When 'Laying Back' is the name,
Procrastination is the game.

HOW ARE WE LIVING OUR LIVES

How are we living our lives,
I mean living from day to day.
Are you seeking out new friends?
Are you finding time to play?

Do you find your temper rises
As the leaves fall from the trees?
Do you still get the feeling come Spring?
Is there awareness of Summer's breeze?

Do you still care what people think
About the things you do?
Would you ever leave work early one day
Just to amble through the zoo?

Do you remember what date it is
Each day of the week?
Have you figured out, from people you know,
Who is strong and who is weak?

Do you really think you're living now?
Well, I'll give you a for-instance.
If, you should stop breathing, right now,
Would you really know the difference?

The only claim to fame you'll have
Is what your close friends make it.
So enjoy yourself, while you can,
Or else, learn how to fake it!

I'M JUST LEARNING

I'm just learning —
That life isn't really
All apple pie, and
There really are people
Who could spit in your eye.

I'm just learning -
That when children grow up,
They set parent traps.
That truth isn't always
A matter of facts!

I'm just learning —
There are negative responses
In most people's minds,
So when seeking more knowledge,
Only faults can they find.

I'm just learning —
That those who are jealous
Eat themselves up alive.
Those who are respectful
Are the ones who'll survive!

I'm just learning —
That the separation of generations
Is a very bad thing.
Happiness means flowing
In a mutual mainstream.

I'm just learning —
Not to tell the whole truth
If it causes disgrace.
And that being sincere
Is a true state of Grace.

I'm just learning —
That listening and learning
To feel what they say
Helps you along
With the games people play!

I'm just learning —
Not to think that I'm finished
Like a book on a shelf.
But improving and contributing
Parts of myself!

GRATEFUL
ACKNOWLEDGEMENTS

Joyce Brand
Patricia Ives
Sharon Griffith . . .
my glorious three

Estelle Wagner
Sarine Lisberg . . .
for support and devotion

Ann Weiner
Sharon Lapin . . .
for inspiration

Robert Ira Schuffman
Marc Ira Levin
Timothy William Schuffman . . .
for laughter and love

About the author . . .

Dolly Schuffman has had a very versatile
life. Although she is not new to writing, this
is her first book of verses.

Her formative years were spent in training
for dance and theater. She is a graduate of
the Chicago Musical College.

During her years in the drama and dancing
field, she was directing, staging, writing
plays, including music and lyrics.

While living in Denver, Colorado, she had
the opportunity to direct a TV show for
new writers.

At present, Dolly and her husband Arthur
reside in Southern California, where her
days consist of running her own Cosmetic
Company. She has been active in the
cosmetic field for over twenty years. She
created Perfection Cosmetics and is the
make-up artist and product developer for
the company.

When asked why she wrote her book, she
said: "For the love of people."